Robert Noble Graham

Published by Robert Noble Graham

www.rngnovels.co.uk

Contents

3 Foreword

4 Soviet Surprises (*Flutters on Aeroflot, menus as fiction and tricky technology in the worker`s Paradise*)

13 Rambling in Rome (*The fun to be had in the Eternal City when you can`t read a map*)

30 Coffee in Cuba (*"The conveyor belt of human beauty" ,the music, the beaches, the cars, the laughter – like nowhere else on earth*)

50 Rhodes (*In the citadel of Knights Templar ,the glory of Karimos, the butterfly farm with no butterflies, the temporary Colossus*)

60 North West Greece (*The ancient Greek Hades, how to become immortal from the knees down, unbelievable Meteora, Parga the jewel in Ionian sunshine*)

About the Author.

Foreword

Travel has always held a particular glamour for me. That`s not the same as saying I have always enjoyed travel. Quite often I`ve found it more of a disruption than I have wanted, but since I have very rarely been forced to go anywhere I have only had myself to blame. Often I have enjoyed it and sometimes more in retrospect than during it. This is a little book about some of the memorable times. Whether it was visiting the ancient Greek underworld, trying to eat bouncing dessert in the old Soviet Union or getting lost in the unlit streets of Cuba, travel has usually brought variety.

I am not the kind of traveller who enjoys discomfort. When I read about Michael Palin in central Africa heading for the toilet at night only to realise something was alive and moving inside it I congratulate myself for liking a decent bed and a good meal. Of course life doesn`t always bring what you want, and I wouldn`t have chosen to float out of my bed during a thunderstorm in Corfu, but accidents happen. This modest work was compiled with the short term traveller in mind. I`ve always loved books where you can read five or six pages which are complete in themselves. I hope it brings amusement and a little instruction.

Some of my travels have been alone. Some with companions. Where I mention Solo`s that is a holiday company for people who are either not in a relationship or whose partner does not want to travel with them (surprisingly common.)

Soviet Surprises

My wife and I had thought we didn't need a summer holiday, but as summer approached and everyone we knew was jetting off somewhere we changed our minds. We went down to the travel agent and the only options left were a trek through malarial swamps in central America which was described in the brochure as `exhilarating` or The Soviet Union. Neither of us could think of a single reason why we would want to visit the USSR but we had decided on a break so we went.

In those days you could only go to the USSR through an agency called Intourist which, we were reliably informed later, was a branch of the KGB. It turned out to be a remarkable and unforgettable experience. The brochure had warned us not to expect the smiling, sexy air stewardesses of Panam or Air France. In the unmistakably clunky prose of Soviet officialdom, it advised that citizens of the USSR do not feel the same need as westerners to bare their teeth at every opportunity, so we should not interpret their tombstone faces (that phrase is mine not aforementioned officialdom) to suggest an absence of the warm and soaring soul of liberated socialist womanhood. This was our first warning that `socialist womanhood` was to leave a deep impression on us during our trip.

The brochure had not warned us about apples. That had not seemed like an omission when we first read it. However, during this holiday we had six flights by Aeroflot, at the time the world's most accident- prone airline. On each flight we were all given an apple. Every single apple had a hole in it. `More organic`, suggested my wife Penny. The arch conspiracy theorist in the group, George, advised that meant a bugging device had been inserted into it. This was 1974 when even James Bond's gadgets bulged in a pocket so this showed remarkable respect for

Soviet technology, a respect not borne out by other experiences during the visit.

We had also not been warned about the joie de vivre of Aeroflot planes. We were not long out of Glasgow when it appeared we were plunging headlong into France. I peeped out of the window and eyeballed a startled Breton on his bicycle on his way for his first pastis of the day, probably a large one. Just as I was rehearsing the French for `we are not seriously injured and we have an apple` the plane betrayed recent advances in Soviet rocketry by pointing straight for the clouds and heading upwards. Penny felt unable to eat her apple or anything else.

Moscow airport, `a modern, thriving hub` according to the brochure, introduced us to a number of aspects of Soviet life. The most memorable was the smell of toilets which contended during our two weeks with overcooked cabbage and diesel as our prime and lingering olfactory experience. The other was queues which appeared not to move or serve any purpose other than to allow Soviet man to be with other Soviet men, none requiring the bourgeois tendency to do something, have an aim, have a coffee and certainly not smile.

Eventually the bus took us to Moscow. Once we had passed the acres of concrete tower blocks we arrived at something else the brochure had not prepared us for: a surprisingly beautiful city. We had heard that Leningrad (now St. Petersburg) was beautiful but no one had told us how varied, impressive and stately were the buildings of central Moscow. At last we had all found a reason to bare our teeth in contemptible western style and give a little smile of relief. Our hotel was just across the square from the Bolshoi theatre (a fact that had escaped the numerous taxi drivers George trusted to give him a tour). It was famous for having hosted meetings between Molotov and Malenkov and

Krushchev and Sholokhov and many other popular heroes of Soviet life. This was the Hotel Metropol.

In the Hotel Metropol we were obliged to queue while a woman with a tombstone face filled up forms which we were obliged to take up to our landing where another ray of feminine sunshine examined them and, apparently, did them all again. We soon learned that these `landing ladies` who occupied large desks on hotel landings day and night were a normal feature of life here. We had assumed they were something to do with room service but this proved not to be true.

It was with some relief that we finally got to our room. It was now getting a little dark so I pressed the light switch. No light came on but the bath started running. We assumed there was a `tombstone` woman in the bathroom preparing to scrub our capitalist bodies within an inch of our lives, but there was not. Simply a wiring fault apparently. We assumed that turning the bath taps on would give us light but it didn`t. It started the bath water running. We wondered if there was any lever or button which would not start the bath running. Mercifully, we found side lamps that worked. Other than that, the room was very spacious and, architecturally, had some style. The view of the square was also impressive. Only later did we find another challenge for the traveller. Every sheet on the bed had a carefully cut and sewn perfectly round hole in it. George had probably concluded it was just the right size for a small pistol to go through. Neither we nor anyone else in our group ever found a purpose for this hole.

We congregated for dinner. We had heard mild warnings about Soviet cuisine so we sat with some trepidation as we awaited our first meal. This gave Fiona and Mike an opportunity to recount their astonishing experience. Apparently a middle-aged American with the same mindset as George occupied the room above them. On inspecting his room for bugs (

you may recall James Bond doing this and neutralising one with a grape) the American noticed a suspicious bulge in the carpet. Triumphantly he rolled back the rug to reveal a dome-like attachment to the floor. Having come prepared, the American undid the large number of screws only to be rather shocked by the sound of a thunderous crash from below. He ran down to find Fiona and Mike staring at the massive chandelier which had plummeted to earth only inches from their heads.

We became accustomed to the similarity between mealtimes at the Metropol and everything we had ever read about limbo. No one appeared. Nothing happened. There was no explanation of what might happen or when that would happen. There was certainly no suggestion of alternative arrangements. When George stormed off to complain he was met with stony indifference by the receptionist followed by the one example of her imperfect grasp of customer relations `You wait. You wait. ` Eventually a door swung open and waiters appeared with trays. On the trays were fritter- like objects with a strange, orange hue. Beside them were potatoes which appeared neither boiled nor mashed and certainly not sautéed. `Disintegrated` was the term suggested by Stephen, who had apparently survived military service in Egypt. This was our first introduction to the abiding character of cuisine at the Metropol. It was not so much indigestible as unidentifiable. A vegetarian would have had a hard time determining which member of the natural world, animal or vegetable had sacrificed itself for this. We ate it. It had, essentially, no flavour, but was at least edible. The same could not be said of desert which was a brightly coloured rectangle with purple and green stripes. Attempts to penetrate it with a spoon propelled it out of the bowl onto the table. Knife and fork had no greater success. We picked it up and attempted to bite it, but it simply sank beneath our teeth and bounced back into place. We asked the waiter what it was. He didn`t know. We advised that we were unable to eat it. He didn`t care.

We slept comfortably enough and had breakfast that we decided to refer to as `mistreated egg`. It had not exactly been scrambled, fried or boiled, simply liberated from its shells and left to fend for itself. Then we had our first excursion. We had two tourist guides, Natasha and Natasha. They both spoke quite good English but were, in the main, impervious to any attempt at fraternisation by us. They were both young and reasonably attractive. The smaller and older of the two did show some hints of a smile on the first day and later became quite sociable and jolly. The taller one continued to regard us as one might view rattlesnakes but even she, later in our stay when far from Moscow in the High Caucasus joined in a singsong and learned a passable version of the Mingulay Boat Song. Their training had obviously consisted of ways of rendering western visitors too brain-dead to ask awkward questions. This was achieved by detailing to us every architect of every building we passed, occasionally punctuated by a rundown on the dates when Lenin had visited the place and what he thought of it. If, by chance, young Zaranov had exceeded his norm during one of these visits it was recorded and celebrated. We were not permitted to know whether his norm concerned steel production, bootlicking or creating plastic puddings for the bourgeoisie.

As we drove through the streets of Moscow we had one of our more telling displays of Soviet womanhood. Modern male tennis lovers whose pulses race on watching delectable Russian ladies like Maria Sharapova would be surprised that no such figures were in evidence for much of our stay. Instead, there was a race of females dedicated to road mending. These `ladies` were large in all directions with, as far as we could tell, few claims to femininity. We wondered if the great worker state had emancipated certain individuals from gender identity and had created this new sex which was not male or female but, perhaps, `feminoid`. Perhaps we should not have been surprised. We had seen similar examples winning Olympic throwing events. On our first free day we went with Fiona and Mike to search out the `vibrant café life` allegedly centred round Nevsky Prospekt. We travelled by the palatial underground, a magnificent monument to the advantages of pitiless slave labour. As we waited, we saw the first of the many citizens stretched out on a bench fully clothed, comatose with an empty bottle of vodka beside him. We saw a couple more as we journeyed, finally arriving at our destination. We soon realised that `vibrant` was not to be confused with `visible` or even `discoverable`. Nevsky Prospekt appeared to consist of drab buildings with dirty windows and poor lighting. Joy descended on us when we passed one hotel which advertised a `tearoom ` on the fifth floor. On leaving the lift we found ourselves in a bright, well upholstered tea room with spacious chairs, flowers and paintings around the walls. We all brightened. I was particularly astonished to see, almost immediately an athletic young man sitting at one table whom I recognised. He returned my gaze with a smile. He obviously did not recognise me but equally obviously was fairly accustomed to my type of reaction. After a moment I said:

"Forgive me for staring. I`ve just realised who you are. You are Pierre Barthes, the French tennis champion." He smiled and nodded his head in confirmation. We had a brief conversation in which he said he was in Moscow for a tournament. He allowed that it was not his favourite tournament. When I said we were relieved and impressed to see such a nice tearoom he did suggest we restrain our optimism.

We took a seat and looked at the menu. It offered `tea with milk, tea with rum, tea with lemon, tea with mint.` We waited and after the mandatory half hour a `feminoid` appeared. We said we'd like tea with lemon.

"No lemon," came the dismissive reply.

"O.K. well we'll have tea with milk"

"No milk."

"Ah, tea with mint"

"No mint."

"Don't suppose there's any rum."

"No rum"

"Do you have any tea?"

"Of course we have tea."

The rest of our two weeks was in similar vein. It had a high point in Leningrad when all 15 of us in the party teamed up with 12 Germans staying in the same hotel for a visit to the Hermitage Museum. This mighty and magnificent building was one of the jewels in the crown of Peter the Great's western capital, a Venice of the Baltic. The Hermitage was considered to be the largest museum in the world (in fact I think the Louvre may be bigger). Our guide, a pleasant looking dark haired lady named Olga smartly led us into the giant building and proceeded to dragoon us through gallery after gallery. "This room has 25 Rembrandts.

This one has 14 French impressionists" Olga never looked back. The fact that some of the group were upwards of 60 if not 80 did not tempt her to slow the pace. We soon realised people were being lost in the vast, endless corridors of priceless art. "Here we have Italian Quattrocento" and on she strode. We were young and determined. Of the 27 who entered 5 of us came out at the other end, exhausted, bored, seized by a hatred for anything cultural. Olga turned, fresh as a daisy, looked pleased with her day`s work if a little surprised to see any of us at all. She said "goodbye" and strode off into the darkening Leningrad streets.

The truth is that it was very hard to view the country fairly. We were taken one day to a presentation where a couple of academics and some kind of functionary gave us `an introduction to Soviet Life`. This informed us that there was no unemployment in the Soviet Union, no crime, no alcoholism and no graffiti. The latter seemed indeed to be true, but we later realised that you couldn`t buy a can of spray paint anywhere in Moscow. That probably reduced the likelihood. We had a chance to ask questions and pointed out that we had seen three obvious drunks lying on benches that day. "These people are not drunks," we were advised. "These people are ill and will be taken care of." We asked if all sick people in the Soviet Union were obliged to carry empty vodka bottles with them but they didn`t hear that question as they rhapsodised about Soviet sporting superiority. We felt that if we persisted with our questions we might be `taken care of` also.

There is no doubt that the Soviet Union did achieve great things and in some cases it managed a level of social cooperation which perhaps eludes us in modern societies. For those who caused no trouble there possibly was a greater level of security and health provision than in many countries. It is also true that the damage

11

inflicted by the Nazis was unspeakable, but the price paid by the people was unacceptable. Life was clearly drab, insecure, fearful and horribly restricted. There was very little to hope for. It is now clear that most people knew they were living amongst lies, but could do nothing about it.

Rambling in Rome

I`ve sometimes wondered what my choice would be if someone offered me the chance to spend six months in just one foreign country. Spain would be a strong candidate. So would Greece. Germany has many attractions. America has great variety, and the Americans are generally friendly and hospitable but I don`t know it well enough and the huge distances would probably disqualify it. I`d want a country that is fairly compact, with generally good weather, likeable people, great cities, good food, beautiful scenery and preferably with a language I speak moderately well. I think the winner would probably be Italy, with Spain as runner-up. One of the many attractions would be the chance to make several trips to Rome. It ranks, for me, in the super-league of the world`s inexhaustibly interesting and enjoyable capitals along with London, New York and Paris. Athens should possibly be added to that list but I don`t know it well enough. However, possibly more than any of the others, Rome is overwhelming. So much in it is breathtaking that the opportunity to escape for a time to the Amalfi coast or the lovely towns of Liguria for tranquillity would be important. Italian friends have told me my view of the country is a little idealised. Its bureaucracy may be infuriating and its politicians often questionable. Its problem of organised crime is obviously dreadful, but the visitor is unlikely to be much troubled by these issues.

I went to Rome for the first time in the month of January some years ago. In summer, like the other Italian cities, it becomes unbearably hot and the tourist crowds make sightseeing much more difficult. In January it can be sunny and mild. During my first visit I don`t think the daytime temperature dropped below 15 degrees Celsius and the sky was usually blue. I had booked into a small hotel in Via Massimo d`Azeglia near the main railway station and the city centre. It was dark when I arrived but still fairly early evening. I was eager to get out and explore. I have often taken rather a foolhardy approach to foreign parts. I like to go out and walk without necessarily planning where I am going. When travelling with others I have usually curtailed that tendency but on my first evening in Rome I gave it free rein. I set off and fairly soon passed the mighty cathedral of Santa Maria Maggiore which I noted for later in the week. Then I passed the Opera House where Simon Boccanegra was playing. On I went to the Via Nazionale. Rome is famously built on seven hills. Well, I was now on the Quirinale hill, but they are not much more than gentle slopes, and I took the downhill direction because I knew that old Rome lay down on the banks of the Tiber.

My first impression was a little disappointing. The street was dark, quiet and unremarkable. However, I walked on. Near the bottom of the slope there was an illuminated area to my left. It was a small excavation taking place just below pavement level. It was mildly interesting, so I tried to console myself that at least I had seen something ancient. Shortly after that I reached a roundabout known as Largo Magnanapoli. To the left was a very wide stairway going downwards. I could just see some light from the bottom of it so I decided to follow it.

Before I got to the bottom of the stairway I was met by the most impressive sight. A few yards in front of me was a high column with the Emperor Trajan on top. He was looking out on the illuminated ruins of the ancient Roman forums. Ahead of him were the excavated remains of temples, great houses, arches and statues. I was standing now on Via dei Fori Imperiali which, to my left, ran all the way to the Colosseum. To my right, past the bulky shadow of ancient buildings, eerily beautiful, was the eternal flame on the great, white, pillared bulk of the monument to Victor Emmanuel, the first king of the united country. Italy only became a united country in 1861 and even then Rome was not part of it. It was still, incredibly, under French rule. However, that changed in 1871 and it has been the nation's capital ever since. The truth is that in daylight this monument is not the most subtle piece of Roman architecture. It has been called `the typewriter` and `the wedding cake` and it does look as if the major building ingredient was icing sugar but as part of the great panorama that greeted me on that first evening it was majestic. The artificial lighting of the ruins in the surrounding darkness lent a timeless quality to the scene. I didn't feel I was in a modern capital city. I was caught in a memory of one of the world's supreme civilisations. Courage, imagination, discipline, selfishness and cruelty were all among the many elements that led to its power. That power is gone, but the aura remains.

I was so exhilarated by this scene that I walked on. Just to my right were the Capitoline Hill where the city was founded, according to legend and beside it the Piazza del Campidoglio, designed by Michelangelo Buonarotti, one of the mighty names closely associated with Rome and Papal power. I wandered off in the other direction, alongside the ruins of the forum to the Colisseum. I strolled on, ready for more dazzling scenes. I was soon a little less ready as the streets became darker and more deserted. I had a rough idea of the layout of the city centre as I walked, but perhaps `rough` is the wrong word. `Wrong` is perhaps a better word because in no time I was lost. I was going along poorly lit avenues with narrow ancient alleys running off them. In daylight these alleys were no doubt quaint and picturesque. By night they made me regret my knowledge of Italian opera which I had previously always considered to be life-enhancing. I found myself remembering Rigoletto and the sinister assassin, Sparafucile, who lurked in dark passages to carry out evil deeds with his stiletto. That took place in Mantua of course, not Rome, and, in fact, it never took place at all since it was a story invented by a Frenchman, Victor Hugo. This did not comfort me much. I also began to realise I was hungry since, in my excitement, I had neglected to eat earlier. I reminded myself, as I had done before, that I should take a closer look at the map before going on such outings. Better still, I should carry the map with me.

A proper travel writer could now tell you which corner of the ancient city he turned to see a welcoming light, but I can`t do that since I was lost. However, this left turn revealed the illuminated sign `Trattoria` just ahead of me. I decided I was going in. However repellent it looked or smelled when I got to it I was going in. I reached the door and could see no one inside. Surely not closed. I opened the door and entered a tiny restaurant with perhaps six tables in all. There were no customers or any sign that any customers had ever been there or were expected. There was however that delicious smell that Italian restaurants the world over seem to concoct. It was an amalgam of garlic, basil, tomatoes and, no doubt, Chianti. This only added to my torment if in fact the place was not serving. However, soon a very small man came out of the back shop. He was scarcely above five feet tall with thinning dark hair and glasses. "Prego signore, posso aiutarle ?"(Please sir, can I help you?) "Aperto?" I asked eagerly(" are you open?") . He smiled broadly and assured me he was. He called out something to someone behind him and an equally small and smiling woman appeared. Like a well-practised stage act they gabbled away to me in Italian, neither seeming to interrupt the other but taking over the explanation at crucial points. I saw how Italian opera was born. Anyone who thinks the duets and quartets of Verdi are artificial needs to visit the dark streets of Rome alone. I didn`t follow all of this remarkable outburst but they seemed to say they had cleared most things away but they had some very fresh fish and spinach if that would be acceptable. "Perfetto, molto accetable," I gabbled in turn, somehow instinctively finding my role in this performance. Perhaps my background in opera was helpful after all. I also negotiated a carafe of local wine and marvelled as work began. I sat at a corner table and a candle was brought which didn`t do much to enhance the soft lighting but added atmosphere. Then came the wine with a little dish of olives and some bread. A few minutes later out came the busy little man again with a small plate of linguine cooked with garlic and cream and sprinkled with parmeggiano. The change in my mood was almost instant. From weary, a little anxious and more than a little annoyed with myself I felt I had walked into the home of long lost relatives who were making a fuss of me. I began to feel good, reminding myself that I loved Italy and congratulating myself on my bold disdain for

17

`neurotic planning`. The reader may like to remember this self-congratulation later in this account.

The fish with spinach was superb. I finished with coffee and paid the absurdly modest bill before we improvised a moving trio of farewells and I left. I took a mental note to revisit the place during my stay. However, although I have been back to Rome on several occasions I have never been able to find it again. It was like one of these magical houses in children`s stories that only appear once every ten years and only when a traveller is in great need. This was typical of Italy as I have known it. In my experience Spain is the only other country where you can wander into the most unassuming of eating places and have confidence that you will dine well.

Alcohol clouds the judgement but after this meal it was for some reason quite obvious to me how I should return to my hotel. In no time I escaped from dark streets and came out near Santa Maria Maggiore. I slept well that night, pleased with my first evening.

I went down for breakfast the following day to find I was the only non-oriental in the room. Although Rome has fewer tourists in January than in the summer it still appeared to have attracted all of Tokyo. I also appeared to be the only non-smoker. The sight of so many Japanese, old and young, male and female, puffing eagerly, even desperately, over cups of coffee was quite disturbing. I have to confess that smoking is a pet aversion of mine. I can understand why human beings do most things but smoking seems to me so completely insane that it bewilders me. I am aware that cultural attitudes differ and within my lifetime this was probably also once acceptable in Britain, but not for some decades. I was tempted to go elsewhere for breakfast but my Scottish blood asserted itself since I had paid for this. I chose a table by the window, opened the window wide and collected my food from the buffet. I noticed a change of tone in the room. I returned to my table to find most of the guests looking at me. One young man came up to me and said: "We are cold." "I have asthma," I replied, which was not strictly true but the smoke was certainly an irritant. Considerable muttering followed. Soon they left. I wondered if this minor confrontation would take place every day.

It was a bright, mild day and I set off to explore. First I had to change some more money and I followed the hotel directions to a `cambio` just round the corner. There was a short queue. As I waited I looked around and my eye was caught by a poster which read:

"You have probably been pickpocketed in Rome by now. If you have not you soon will be. Be safe. Buy our Travellers` Cheques."

This was disconcerting but it was certainly a powerful advert. Nonetheless, I changed money and set off. I had brought my sketch pad and decided I would revisit the Forum area in daylight and eventually try to draw something meaningful. The Via Nazionale looked quite different now. It was lively and bustling and I was surrounded by the lovely Italian language. I do think it is the most musical language I have ever heard. I once witnessed a discussion between a traffic warden and an irate motorist in Florence and it was like a scene from Puccini.

19

I returned to Trajan's column and went on to see the Capitoline Museum which is a small collection compared to the immense Vatican museums but the exhibits are magnificent. There is a most impressive statue of the philosopher Emperor Marcus Aurelius on horseback, John the Baptist by the wonderful Caravaggio and the Etruscan statue of the she-wolf suckling the twins Romulus and Remus, mythical founders of the city. This is really just another re-telling of the ancient `twins` myth that turns up in so many mythologies like Baldur and Hod, Jacob and Esau and probably Christ and Judas. It was ancient man's attempt to understand the apparent death of the sun, the bringer of good things, at the summer solstice, leaving heaven to the dark brother until the moon(symbolised in this myth by the she-wolf) suckles the tiny sun child in the depths of winter that becomes the full grown sun god again.

This took most of the morning so by early afternoon I decided to do some sketching. I had decided my first effort would be Julius Caesar's Forum. It is a little less ruined than some of the others from which it sits apart. I had read that Caesar was troubled by the oppressive summer heat in central Rome and opted for a higher location to be cooler. This explanation was a little hard to accept since the difference in altitude is minimal. Reports of him suggest he was not much troubled by cold and I concluded that this perhaps accounted for most of these remarkable expeditions he undertook. As Rome's temperatures rose, he probably began to long for a snowy ditch in the mountains somewhere north. No doubt Calpurnia was quite relieved to hear him announce: "Just off to Transalpine Gaul for a few months dear. I'll bring you back one of these Gaulish cooking pots you like for the garden.

20

I settled at a stone bench in bright sunshine and took out my pad and pencils. I had hardly begun when I was aware of someone approaching. I looked up to see a small, elderly Japanese man carrying a little case. He was smiling and quite unmistakably heading towards me. I assumed he was going to try to sell me something, but I couldn`t imagine what could be in the little case. He looked at my pad and his smile broadened. He pointed at my rudimentary sketch and said something in Japanese which, I assumed, was not: "Well, that`s the best piece of drawing I`ve seen this week," but could have been: "you must be kidding, sunshine." Or "Let me sell you a box of matches to burn that rubbish." I smiled and nodded as if I couldn`t have put it better myself. He then marched off to the next stone bench which was a few yards nearer to Caesar`s Forum, opened his case and took out a pad and box of paints. He held up the pad for me to see like a conjuror about to turn it into a flock of pigeons and pointed to it with more smiles. Again I nodded and smiled. Then we both got down to serious work. Since the forum was already a ruin I felt I didn`t have to be too precise about lines and proportions. Poor as I am at drawing, I am amazed at how satisfying it is. Occasionally I do something that is not terrible and then I swell with pride. The other surprising aspect of what should be the most solitary of activities is how many contacts I make. All sorts of people who would not normally speak to me come up, inspect my drawing and chat to me. A whole Spanish family sat down beside me once in Seville and extracted most of my life story. A wistful German professor in the Luxembourg Gardens in Paris sat down and offered to share his sandwiches when he discovered I spoke his language. His interest in my drawing appeared to be nil but it had still acted as an invisible signpost that I could be approached safely and provided with his melancholy company.

The little Japanese finished before I did and brought his pad over for me to inspect. He had done a very passable water colour of Trajan`s column which was just ahead of us. He then flicked through pages to show me the Rialto Bridge in Venice, the Ponte Vecchio in Florence and the bay of Naples with Capri and Vesuvius. It was really quite impressive and I think I managed to convey that to him. He took another look at my pad and no doubt satisfied himself that the box of matches was the answer. He wandered off in good spirits and I felt as pleased as if we had chatted over a beer.

Breakfast the following morning was something of a revelation. I came down to an empty room. I was compiling my meal, assuming the Japanese had all set off on an early excursion when a couple of their young men came in to fill their coffee cups. One smiled at me and said: "We smoke in other room." He pointed across the corridor where I could make out some of his countryman surrounded by a thick fog. I was stunned and a little ashamed. I told him I was very grateful. They both gave a little smiling bow and shot back off.

After breakfast I wandered off without much of an aim. I simply wanted to see Rome. Almost by chance I happened upon the Trevi Fountain. Rather like the Eiffel Tower, it has appeared in so many films and brochures that it was something of a shock to see that it really existed. I went on to the magnificent Spanish steps and since that is beside some of the main outlets for Bulgari, Armani, Versace and others the always impressive

Italian dress sense becomes as much a feature as the great fountains and churches. I reached the Tiber which looked a little muddy and sluggish, not perhaps the great torrent I had expected. Beyond it was the Castel Sant` Angelo, austere and military. Originally Hadrian`s mausoleum, it had been military headquarters and a prison. Allegedly, it had a secret passage leading to the Vatican for days when the Pope felt divine protection was not quite adequate and a quick sprint to a stout fortress would meet the need. For opera lovers its rooftop was the site of poor Cavaradossi`s firing squad exit and the subsequent leaping of Tosca from the battlements.

It was probably the following day when my wanderings took me into the Colisseum. Again, it is `iconic` so you could not leave Rome without visiting it. The more you know about it the more hideous its story becomes. To go to such trouble and expense to build an amphitheatre for the express purpose of tearing humans and animals apart doesn`t appear to sit easily with the image of Rome as the centre of the civilised world. Those who feel television and shopping have corrupted us all should reflect a little on human pastimes of bygone ages. They were normally unspeakable. Periclean Athens had the great dramatists, Aeschylus, Sophocles, Aristophanes and Euripides to entertain them but that was exceptional. Eighteenth century Britain had bear baiting and dog fighting. France sold tickets to rich people to watch cats being roasted alive. I was reflecting on all this gloom when I noticed there was one other visitor to the huge arena. It was my little Japanese painter friend, at first lost in thought just like myself. We waved and smiled.

After the Colisseum I decided I needed a coffee. I was heading up to the Esquiline hill to see the mighty statue of Moses by Michelangelo in the church of San Pietro in Vincola (Saint Peter in Chains). Just at the top of the steps leading up from the Via dei Fori Imperiali there was a little café. It looked small but colourful and inviting. I went in to be regaled by the wonderful smell of good Italian espresso. Two men around middle age, one lean, bald and sharp- featured and the other more of a pudding, stood behind counters, one to my left and the other to my right. When I went in they were talking in loud voices and gesticulating. I wondered if I was interrupting a vendetta, but soon realised it was reasonably good humoured. "Prego signore," said the bald one. I ordered a coffee and one of the tempting pastries on display. "Sit down," he said in English in a tone that invited obedience. I sat at the window and enjoyed the view down the street and back to the Forum. Almost immediately their conversation resumed. They spoke too rapidly for me to follow much of it and with deep passion. I heard the names Baggio, Viale, Berlusconi, Pasolini, Moravia, Bergonzi and others fired like machine gun bullets across this little scene. It annoyed me that I couldn`t follow it better. What conversation could possibly include two top footballers, a vigorous but questionable rising politician, a recently murdered film director, a major novelist and a splendid operatic tenor? I longed to ask, but nothing in their speech or manner suggested they were at all aware I still existed. The pastry was delicious and the coffee excellent. A small, elderly local walked in. He had a battered brown hat pushed down almost to his ears, thin-rimmed spectacles and the droopiest of handlebar moustaches. A coffee was placed in front of him without, as far as I could tell, his having ordered it.

24

Almost immediately he slid effortlessly into this conversation, all shouting at deafening decibels just like the quartet in "La Forza del Destino" without, as yet, swords drawn. I decided I needed another shot of this first rate caffeine. I saw no alternative but to shout "scuse". Suddenly all went quiet and three sets of astonished Italian eyes settled on me. "Ancora uno café, per favore," I managed boldly. The machine gun exchange resumed and I had no idea whether my request had been registered. I sat feeling very foreign but was gratified to have another espresso placed in front of me with no interruption to the conversation.

The following day after breakfast I decided it was time to take on the Vatican and St.Peter`s. I had a full day to do it so I decided to walk. I wanted to go through the Piazza Campo de `Fiori (The square of the field of flowers) and cross the Tiber at the Ponte Garibaldi. Then, according to the map, it was a simple matter of finding the Via Aurelia and I would reach St.Peter`s. I wanted to climb the 420 steps and see the marvellous view from the top. As always, it was a delight to walk through the old city. Round every corner there was another magnificent fountain and another delightful café. Crossing the river took me to the area known as Trastevere (which, imaginatively, means `across the Tiber`). Much of that area is very old and has some of the best restaurants. Although it was still quite early I stopped in it and had an excellent seafood risotto served by a thin, young waiter who looked like Rowan Atkinson with a tiny goatee beard. He did his job well, but every sentence he uttered was preceded by a deep sigh as if it broke his heart to see this marvellous food wasted on a `mere Brit` who, famously, would have no capacity to appreciate it. To be fair to him, he said and did nothing to imply this was the source of his misery but I found it difficult to believe he spent his entire working life in this mood.

I set off again in bright sunshine. I got a little lost in the network of roads but was heartened when I saw the words Via Aurelia. The map had suggested I would have the choice of going either east or west but, for a reason that was not obvious to me, only westward was on offer. I took it and enjoyed the buildings and fountains of traditional Rome. I had not really expected my small map to be to scale, but the road was seeming a little longer than I had expected. I became more uneasy as the style of buildings changed from traditional, stone-built Italian to what I would term `council-house contemporary`. I concluded from the stares of the children in the street that this was perhaps not the most frequented tourist route in the city. I checked the map and indeed Via Aurelia was the road I needed. On I trudged, conscious that it was some time since I had seen a sign indicating San Pietro, Santa Maria in Trastevere or indeed anything at all. Well, if signs were what I wanted I soon had my wish. As I turned the next corner I was faced with a thundering motorway with a sign pointing north to Florence and another south to Naples. Where the hell was Rome? How could I have mislaid one of the world`s great cities. I looked around and realised I could no longer see the dome of Saint Peter`s. If you are in Rome and cannot see Saint Peter`s then you are blindfolded. Somehow, I had walked out of the great city. I looked again at the name of the road. Via Aurelia Antica. Ah, had I not paid enough attention? Was this a different road and not simply an older part of the same one? I looked at my map with more attention. Via Aurelia was an entirely different road. I had no choice but to turn back.

It took me well over an hour to retrace my steps but eventually I found myself in the Vatican City. My detour had added around ten miles to my stroll. After that, did I still feel like climbing the 420 steps to the top? I decided to look inside Saint Peter`s first. Most of us have seen the huge building and its square on television at papal events or in films like "Angels and Demons". It is still hard to appreciate just how immense it all seems in reality. The size, the cost, the amount of stone, the number of builders and craftsmen, everything about it is on a gigantic scale. Then, when you go into the basilica there seems no end to it. You could fly Concorde through it. Did it give me a sense of the spiritual, the divine? Not really. I have had that feeling much more strongly in small, silent churches in the Highlands of Scotland. No doubt it all depends on your conception of divinity, if you have one. St. Peter`s unquestionably gives the sense of colossal material and earthly power. Near the entrance, on the right, is a booth protected by strengthened glass. Inside it is the pieta of Michelangelo from 1499. For me, it is one of the most affecting of his creations. The fact that solid marble can be made to look so delicate that Mary`s dress seems like soft material is astonishing in itself. She looks young and fragile which is, of course, not realistic if the son lying across her lap died at the age of 33 and she lived under the hot sun of the Middle East. However, as a representative of an eternal feminine principle of tenderness and beauty she is perfect. The expression on her face and the gesture of her hands give a powerful message that is difficult to put into words. To me, she is saying "why do such things need to happen?" and that is a question we still ask with equal force but perhaps with less conviction that there could be any answer.

I then decided I was going to climb the steps. In fact they were not particularly steep so the climb was not demanding. I imagine that in summer this rooftop is crowded. When I reached it I thought at first I was alone. After a few moments I noticed there was one other person, a small man. Yes, it was my Japanese artist friend. We waved and smiled. The views of the great city are magnificent and I was pleased I had made the effort. I could not then leave St. Peter`s without queuing to see the Vatican museums and the Sistine chapel. In summer the queues for this go on for miles. Fortunately, since it had already been a long day I only had to wait for twenty minutes. I don`t know how many visits you would have to make and how long you would have to stay to do justice to the museums. They are immense and they contain treasures from innumerable countries and ages. I joined the crowds slowly ambling from one gigantic, vaulted passageway to the next with huge tapestries on the walls and display cabinets of jewellery, pottery and artefacts alongside us. The goal of course was the Sistine Chapel and the great mural which Pope Julius the second commissioned Michelangelo to paint. Once there, I was tired. The room was crowded and noisy despite the attempts of the ushers to ensure silence. I had seen too much that was overwhelming and splendid. Instead of lifting my spirit and making me aware of eternity it made me realise how much I wanted to have a seat and a coffee and think of an atmospheric trattoria by the Tiber, some excellent Italian cuisine and a glass of decent wine. Rome had defeated me.

I have been back to Rome and hope to return again. Each visit so far has been a kaleidoscope of experiences: the friendly, humorous people, the art treasures, the towering buildings, the

28

sunny weather, the beautiful language, the crowds, the sights of everyday Roman life being lived amongst epic history, temporal power and artistic marvels. I end up overwhelmed as if my soul has spent a week in an ethereal gymnasium, being stretched, toned, massaged and exercised until, like an athlete recovering from supreme efforts I stop and gradually, over weeks and months absorb all that I have seen. Eventually, inspired and uplifted, I feel I have not done justice to any of it and must return.

Coffee in Cuba

Graham Greene described Cuba as `a conveyor belt of human beauty`. That alone would entice many a visitor, but the island has plenty of other charms. I visited there in 1999 with my friend, Mary, who turned out to be an excellent travelling companion, especially when things did not go as planned, a fairly regular experience. Perhaps the final trigger for both of us was seeing that wonderful film: "The Buena Vista Social Club." It says a lot about the island and its uniqueness.

We flew to Havana in May of that year. There were many reasons for each of us to want to visit the island and I had consulted a specialist company to design a visit for us that would enable us to see a good variety of what Cuba has to offer. That included giving us a chance to appreciate the Hemingway connection. Ernest Hemingway lived in Cuba for twenty years towards the end of his life. He had his own boat, Pilar, and went fishing for the spectacular marlin in the Keys. I had resisted the Hemingway allure as a teenager, but discovered him relatively late in life as a very fine writer (perhaps a surprisingly obvious comment but a lot of the razzmatazz around him has very little to do with his books).

This was also the second communist dictatorship I had visited, the first being the USSR many years before. I had read a lot about Fidel Castro and his revolution. Even so, I don`t feel equipped to pass much of a judgement on the man. He has certainly done some terrible things, but his revolution of 1959 took an island that was in the grip of the Mafia, widespread disease and almost universal illiteracy and rendered it free of all three of these plagues. At the time we visited it was one of the safest parts of the planet, partly because of the extraordinary ratio of police to citizens. The health service is celebrated, having done wonderful things for public health on a budget that would not take the NHS very far. As a young man Castro was something of an All American boy. It is tragic that the fears and stubbornness on both sides has impoverished Cuba while doing very little to help the US. Having said all of that, the `feel` of Cuba could hardly have been different from that of Russia. The Cuban people appear to have indestructible self-esteem and merriment. One fact that summed them up for me was learning that the Conga, a dance whereby everyone moves in a line, one behind the other, came into being as the only dance the slaves could do when chained together. How many people would feel like dancing when chained up and in slavery? An interesting, possibly unique, feature for a dictatorship was that we saw no portraits of Fidel, nothing of the `dear leader`or `father of the nation` propaganda beloved of North Korea, Saddam`s Iraq or Mao`s China. What we did see were lots of photographs of Che Guevara. Very reminiscent of my student days in Glasgow when not to have a portrait of Che made you a very suspicious person.

We stayed in the Ambos Mundos hotel in old Havana, a fine hotel in a very beautiful and atmospheric city. It has suffered badly from Cuba`s devastating poverty since the collapse of its patron, The Soviet Union, in the early `nineties. Fortunately, it has been adopted as a World Heritage site and its grand colonial buildings are being restored. The hotel was modern and comfortable and the staff had the smiling ease we came to associate with Cubans. We made the mandatory visit to room 511 where, the story goes, Hemingway wrote most of "For Whom the Bell Tolls." It had his typewriter and some photographs and was perhaps worth seeing. We breakfasted in the rooftop restaurant which gives fine views over the city. You can have a close look at it without journeying to the Caribbean by watching the James Bond film "Die Another Day" where Pierce Brosnan turns up in his pursuit of the North Korean bad guy. We were under no such pressure.

We went out and explored. The city has lots of grand buildings in various states of repair or ruin but altogether it has the feel of an important Spanish city which has seen happier times. The streets were busy apparently at all hours of the day and night and a visitor has to get accustomed quite soon to being recognised as a potential source of dollars which they request good-naturedly, often offering something in return. We had our first serious example of this when we went in for a coffee soon after arrival. Cuban coffee is very good. It is strong but not bitter, almost with a chocolate quality about it. No sooner had we begun to drink than four musicians appeared and sang `Dos Gardenias, ` `Guantanamera` and `Chissa, chissa, chissa`. The performance was very good and we congratulated ourselves in so quickly finding a venue to hear live Cuban music. Music is of course the soul of Cuba. I remember seeing a television programme about the jazz trumpeter, Dizzy Gillespie, who visited the island as often as he could to listen. It was obvious the musicians were targeting us as `wealthy` visitors and we cheerfully paid a dollar for a CD of their performance which, on returning home, we

32

discovered to be blank. Salaries in Cuba were very low indeed. A teacher told us his income was nine dollars a month. Even with the low price of food and the lack of consumer goods that would not buy very much so an additional dollar was treasure to them. We didn`t mind this particularly but by the time you`ve handed out twenty five dollars in a morning it begins to feel like money.

We walked along the broad pedestrian area where smiling black or Hispanic waiters invite you politely, often jokingly, to sample their fare. We strolled along the Malecon, the wide boulevard that runs by the sea where little groups of men sat hopefully with fishing rods, mostly smoking the huge cigars that seemed permanently attached to all Cuban mouths. We saw plenty of the famous cars: the magnificent old Pontiacs and Buicks left here before the revolution by wealthy Americans. They are treated with great love and constant care. If Cuban men are not fishing they are likely to be gathered under the bonnet of a Cadillac fitting some component from a washing machine or vacuum cleaner that miraculously makes the car go. Graham Greene`s words about the conveyor belt of beauty came easily back to mind. The young women did not have the money to wear high fashion, but they had unquestionable natural beauty, rhythm and elegance. The men, in a country with no expensive gyms or sports centres mostly looked as if they could step into a ring with Muhammad Ali or Tyson at their peak. The horrific natural selection that was the slave trade had resulted in a race of physically magnificent people. Another point confirmed to us again and again is that there appeared to be no tension between the races. Whites, Hispanics and Blacks appeared to live and deal with each other quite happily.   Later that afternoon when we

33

were hot and a little worn we made our way to one of the Hemingway shrines in Havana, La Floridita, not so much because of associations with Ernest but because it was near our hotel and we were thirsty. We were probably a little under his influence since we drank daiquiris. They are made with crushed ice, rum, lime juice, maraschino and sugar. Very refreshing but we didn`t try for Hemingway`s alleged record of 16 at a sitting. As we relaxed in the very pleasant atmosphere with our excellent drink three musicians appeared and sang `Dos Gardenias,` `Guantanamera` and `Chissa, chissa, chissa`. What a coincidence, we thought as we handed over a dollar for another CD which turned out not to be blank.

We had our first encounter that evening with Cuban cooking. The restaurants are state-owned and seemed to feel no great pressure to prepare anything very enjoyable. Rather oily chicken legs with white rice and beans appeared quite often in our stay. We soon learned that the way to eat a little better is to hang around your hotel lobby until someone quite shifty and suspicious sidles up to you and asks if you would like a decent meal. This is how you find a *Paladar*. These are private houses which are licensed to feed up to twelve people at a time in return for payment. We decided to take a chance on this on our second evening in Havana and had some very acceptable fish. As we were to discover, this method is not always such a good idea. I had an encounter with another aspect of Cuban life the following day. We had lunch in a reasonable restaurant beside the famous theatre where their highly regarded ballet troupe trains. Mary went off to the toilet and I decided to find out where we could buy some of the very good fruit we had sampled at breakfast. That was the one meal that was well done. Delicious, very fresh mangoes, papayas and pineapples were available along with quite reasonable omelettes. I asked one of the waitresses who looked a little uncertain since she didn`t actually live close by. At that moment a very beautiful black teenager came by and the waitress asked her if she could help. The young lady looked at me with large, clear eyes  and said she could happily take me to a good shop close by and then `we could spend some time together`. I don`t think I was misunderstanding the message and I was certainly not impervious to the attraction, but I was actually quite relieved when Mary joined us and the moment passed.

Another idea which turned out not to be so good was hiring a car. We had booked hotels in Havana, Trinidad de Cuba, across the island from Havana on the Caribbean side, Santiago in the south, Cuba`s second city, and the tobacco growing area in the north, Pinar del Rio. We were not driving to Santiago. Cuba is almost 900 miles long and the drive from Havana, judging by our Trinidad experience, would have taken the rest of our lives. We were doing that one by plane but car for the others. It seemed quite reassuring at first. The cars were quite modern. The staff were helpful. They provided us with a 24 hour helpline number. This was before the days when mobile phones were common and it did not occur to us that a 24 hour helpline is not much use on an island with almost no telephones. The next challenge was that Havana is quite a large city without many road signs. It also proved impossible to find a map other than a very sketchy tourist one. We had no idea how to get out of Havana to reach the six lane highway which, we knew, crossed the island to Trinidad. I had an inspiration. I would ask a taxi driver. Mary thought this an excellent idea. I chose one parked outside our hotel and, in typically Cuban style, he took the time to give me considerable detail about the road to follow.

We set off merrily at nine in the morning. The journey, we knew, should take about four hours. Mary navigated carefully, and after just over half an hour we reached the edge of the city. Unfortunately, as we soon discovered, it was the wrong edge. We were in the northern not the western edge which was the one we needed. The directions were rubbish. We decided we could do it if we just drove back in to the centre and then took the first big road on the right. This plan took us through a remarkable part of Havana with sumptuous high rise buildings. This evidently was the area built by the Mafia to house their casinos, dance halls and night clubs. Interesting as that was, it didn`t help us to find our road. After wasting two hours like this we decided the only hope was to head south on the highway to Varadero and then find a connection to the motorway. I was amazed at how calmly Mary accepted this gamble.

 We headed inland and were soon driving past sugar cane fields on either side. We had escaped from the city and felt we deserved a coffee to restore us. However, this was not Europe or America and service stations were not on offer. Our problems multiplied when we encountered one of the dangers of Cuban roads: potholes. We had a puncture. In itself that was a delay, not a disaster. It occurred to us, however, to wonder what we would do if we had another puncture. We had now used the spare and in our hours of travelling we had not seen a single garage. We drove on in a thoughtful mood and came to a village. I suggested we stop for coffee but Mary was hesitant. We saw very large black men at bars and cafés. There was no sign of tourists or any facilities for tourists. The men were presumably workers in the sugar plantations. Frankly, the scene looked so alien and foreign that Mary did not want to stop and I felt a little the same way. We were a little ashamed of this but things had not gone well that day so we continued.

A little further on we decided we should stop and rest our legs. There was a pleasant little green space by the side of the road with a bench and some trees for shade. We had a couple of mangoes with us and decided we deserved them. We sat down and enjoyed the delicious fruit, but were somewhat surprised a couple of minutes later when three musicians appeared and sang `Dos Gardenias,` `Guantanamera` and `Chissa, chissa, chissa`. We bought the CD. Where they had sprung from and where they disappeared to we didn`t know. "Are mangoes hallucinogenic?" Asked Mary

Since we had no proper map and there were no road signs we could only hope that we would eventually reach the six-lane highway we had read about. Our concerns rose still further when, as we climbed a hill, the car began to lose power and we drifted to a halt. I checked the petrol but we still had plenty. I know almost nothing about cars anyway so even if I had known how to lift the bonnet I hadn`t much idea what should be under it. If I found a dead horse I would identify that as a problem, but I thought that unlikely. Since neither of us had any other idea and the 24 hour helpline was seeming like a poor joke my only suggestion was to try turning the key in the ignition. To our huge relief it started as if nothing was wrong. This sequence of events was repeated several times over the next few days until we found a dealer in one of the towns. He checked the car and said it was fine. When I pressed him on the problem he had an idea: "Did you have the air conditioning on?" "Yes, of course. It was hot and that`s why we wanted an air-conditioned car." He smiled knowingly. "The car won`t go when the air-conditioning is on," he triumphantly explained. Apparently our choice was to sit comfortably in the middle of Cuba with pleasant air conditioning but go nowhere or drive in sweltering conditions with the windows open.

Nine hours after our departure from Havana we reached the Caribbean coast and the town of Cienfuegos. This was a huge relief. We found a hotel which could serve us coffee but no food unless we wanted a full meal. We did, but we were booked in for one at Trinidad which was now only a few miles away. The waiter considerately supplied some small tapas which went down well. Cienfuegos means "one hundred fires" and is the home town of the wonderful musician, Compay Segundo. On another day we would have spent time finding out why it had this strange name and where Compay had lived, but we had metamorphosed from intrepid, eager tourists to pathetic beings who just wanted to stop driving. We set off again, hoping that no other obstacle would delay us. In fact, one did, but it was not one that caused us distress. A couple of miles from our destination we noticed something moving on the surface of the road ahead of us. The `something` was pink. In fact, it turned out to be many `somethings`. They were little land crabs which had come down a mountain stream and were crossing to the sea. It was obvious from the corpses on the road that quite a lot came to grief. We later discovered that their standard reaction, heroic but foolhardy, on seeing traffic approach was to stop, confront the car and show their pincers. We tried to shepherd some across and build a tiny, temporary wall to delay the others so we could pass without damaging any. Not sure if we succeeded.

Soon we reached the beautiful town of Trinidad de Cuba. Our hotel, La Cueva, was like a very luxurious African village. Our room was actually a little, free standing house with a thatched roof. Inside it was modern, comfortable, clean and cool. We were so relieved. At first we were almost too tired and hungry to feel like eating, but we had a shower followed by a beer and then enjoyed a reasonable piece of fish. The following morning Mary wanted to rest so I strolled into the town. Trinidad dates back to the 16th century and the old colonial buildings are in excellent condition. As I walked along, many of the inhabitants were either sitting at their front door, working at some craft or chatting to neighbours. Almost without exception they smiled and wished me good day. A couple of the men wanted to talk and we conversed about where I came from and what I was going to see. I expected the conversation to end with a suggestion that I supply a dollar or that I listen to a rendition of "Dos gardenias" etc., but that didn`t happen. I noticed that several houses were offering accommodation for one dollar a night. I wondered if I would ever have the courage to try such a visit but so far I never have.

Since we were on the Caribbean coast I had my first experience of scuba diving which was beautiful. Then we hired a guide for the supposedly strenuous walk into the interior to the Salto del

Caburni waterfall. Our guide was a very charming English teacher who could make more on a day`s guiding than in a month of teaching. The walk was hilly and we went through some dense undergrowth, but it was relatively gentle and our companion was splendid. Eventually I did press him a little about how he felt about Castro and the country`s relative isolation. Understandably, he was cautious but eventually recited a number of the pros and cons. He reckoned they might lose as much as they gain when the inevitable reintegration with the western world came about. Life could be rather austere as things were, but there was a lot of mutual support and personal security. "Once the boatloads come over from Florida", he sighed, "we`ll have consumer goods and crime."

Our drive back to Havana was mercifully uneventful apart from the last hour when we were supposed to find a place at the airport to leave the car. Again the directions we had been given seemed to make no sense even to a policeman at the airport. With only minutes to spare we finally found a minute Portakabin where a merry Hispanic set us free.

In Santiago, we stayed in the Casa Granda, the 1920s hotel in which Graham Greene had stayed when writing much of `Our Man in Havana`. It is very central, looking out on a large square where you can watch the citizens come and go as you enjoy a daiquiri in the downstairs bar that looks out to the square. After our rather hectic journey there we decided to do just this. The bar was spacious in grand colonial style and the waiter, a passable lookalike for Muhammad Ali, was friendly, good-humoured and efficient. This was around six in the evening and we noticed the square was gradually filling up with giggling, well-dressed young women. We asked the waiter why and he simply raised his eyebrows and smiled a little wearily. Soon we realised why. The girls were calling to the men in the bar, offering to give them a good time in Santiago.

As we made our way back to our room a young man whom I had noticed watching us sidled up and asked if we would like a decent meal on our stay. Since the Havana experience had really been quite good we decided to accept. His name was Alejandro and we agreed he would turn up on our third evening and take us to the chosen Paladar. He also told us he ran the tourist bureau a couple of streets away and we should call in if we wanted anything.

 We had a good night and an excellent breakfast again on the rooftop. We then took a taxi the six miles out to the Castle of San Pedro de la Roca on the coast. This impressive fortification was built in the sixteenth century as a lookout and protection against pirates. We asked the taxi driver if he could come back for us in, perhaps, an hour and a half. He said he would simply wait. We assured him we wouldn`t take any other taxi but he insisted he would wait. We offered him money for what he had done so far but he refused and said he was content to be paid at the end. We strolled off in the sunshine and enjoyed the castle. It seemed very well built and in excellent condition. It tops a hill overlooking the strait between Cuba and Jamaica to the West, Haiti to the East. Simply as a place to sit and enjoy Cuba it was very pleasant. We should have brought a bottle of wine and sandwiches we felt. Of course there was the constant threat of three musicians popping up to sing "Dos Gardenias "etc. We were only a few miles along the coast from Guantanamo which now has more disturbing resonances. At the time, it was simply the home region of the "guajira Guantanamera" the peasant girl addressed by the "truthful man" in Jose Marti's lovely song which we still liked a lot despite its frequent renditions.

Later we walked in the streets of Santiago. It lies at the foot of the Sierra Maestre mountains, and is a little cut off from the rest of the island. That is no doubt part of the reason why it is so different from the rest that we had seen. Again, although apparently as comfortably multiracial as elsewhere we could not help noticing that many of the black people were more black than any we had ever seen before. We soon realised this was in part because Haiti was just across the water and many Haitians had swum or floated as desperately to Cuba as Cubans had to Florida. The history of French colonisation of Haiti is a truly dreadful story which reflects no credit at all on France past or present. With all its shortcomings I am certain Cuba has been a far better home. We concluded that the slaves taken to Haiti had been from a different tribe than those in Cuba, probably from French colonies rather than Spanish.

Later we found Alejandro in his tourist office where he looked nervous. He eagerly began to tell us how much he wanted email contacts in Europe to conduct `his business`. We were unable to determine quite what this business was and were certainly not keen to hand out email contacts, even if we could have remembered any. We finally prevailed upon him to adopt his role as tourist adviser. Amongst other things we wanted to know where we could find a good café. He gave us directions which we followed. This was a peculiar experience. We found the café and went in. It was quite full. However, when we entered everyone stopped talking and complete silence descended. Mary turned to me and said "we are the only white faces here." We had the strong sense that we were intruding but on the other hand it was an interesting situation. A tall, young man behind the counter smiled and said: "would you like coffee?" "Yes, we would," said Mary bravely. All eyes were on us. We looked around but could not see a spare table. A young man in a baseball cap spoke up. "You can sit here," he said. There were two spare seats at the table where he sat with a friend. We joined them and began to chat in a mixture of English and Spanish. They wondered if we were American, very unlikely since the US government makes it very difficult for its citizens to visit. Some come through the Dominican Republic but not many at that time. Very soon we were drawing maps of the UK and pointing to Scotland. "No, Liverpool is not in Scotland," we explained."The Beatles come from here." Soon most of the café went back to their conversations. The coffee was excellent and the company interesting.

We walked back to our hotel, quite satisfied. As we got nearer to it we heard the sound of music. This time it was not the three standards we had come to expect. This was captivating stuff. Just before our hotel was the most famous music club in Santiago, perhaps in Cuba. For a dollar you could go in and listen for hours to an endless stream of great music. Oddly, without paying a dollar you could stand in the street and enjoy the same thing since there was no wall between the club and the outside world.

43

There was simply a large opening with bars. We went in, paid our dollar and heard a huge variety of great performances in a wonderful atmosphere. While there we were handed fliers for a club a few steps further up the road where we could have music, dancing and drinks from 10.30. We decided to go. That turned out to be one of our better decisions. After dinner we went a little apprehensively along the dark street and down steps to a cellar. However, the cellar was bright and cool. There were tables and a bar, a dance floor and a small band just beginning to tune up. We took daiquiris, sat back and heard some of the most melodic, most rhythmical, happiest music we`ve ever heard. I looked around and reckoned most of the patrons were local. There were several tables where middle-aged white males sat with stunning black teenage girls. We had no doubt it was love. Whether it was love of one`s soul mate, money or the delusions of age and youth we did not know. Some of the Cubans got up to dance and that was a treat. These people could dance. Effortless, joyful, amazingly spontaneous movement just seemed so natural to them. Later we got up and showed them that a nation could have conquered two thirds of the earth with stiff joints and clunky footwork.

The following evening was our last in Santiago and it was when we had arranged to go to a Paladar recommended by Alejandro. Mary told me she wasn`t feeling very well and preferred not to go. Later I discovered she just didn`t trust Alejandro and with some reason. I went down and waited at the bar. Eventually I heard him calling to me from outside. Clearly he didn`t want to be seen in the hotel for some reason. I had stupidly assumed the Paladar would be nearby but we walked further and further from the hotel through streets with almost no lighting. Eventually, he took me up a stair to a sparsely furnished flat with two elderly ladies. One wore an apron and showed me to a kitchen table with a faded waxcloth cover and a knife and fork. Alejandro asked for the two dollar fee we had agreed. I paid him a little grudgingly and he shot off, leaving me in this bleak flat with two old ladies. The one with the apron brought me a glass of water and then a plate with one greasy chicken leg, white rice and a few black beans, pretty much what I would have got in one of the state restaurants for about half the three dollars I paid. I realised I had been swindled and Mary`s intuition had been right. However, that was not my major worry. I had stupidly assumed Alejandro would lead me back to the hotel. Of course, that was not going to happen. After this dismal repast I went down to the street. It was dark with some light coming from a crescent moon. At either end of it I could see small groups of men, some well over six feet tall. They were really just rather large shadows where I could make out broad shoulders and little else. I had not the faintest idea which direction to take. My impression of Cubans up to now had been that they were friendly and honest, but human nature is human nature. I certainly could not see any police presence and I was aware that for many Cubans I was a walking treasure chest. Then I realised that in the distance I could hear music. I felt sure it was coming from the club around from our hotel. I had to follow it. It seemed to me I should go left. Either way I had to pass one of the groups of men and I tried to fight back the question in my mind of why there was a group at either end, making it impossible for me to leave without passing one. At least they were not moving towards me. I set off as boldly as I could, trying to remember what I looked like when I knew where

45

I was going. As I strode on and came near to one of the groups they stopped talking and a couple of them looked at me. "Me gusta la musica" (I like the music) I shouted as nonchalantly as I could. They laughed. I felt sure the laugh was friendly. "Si, si, buena musica acqui" (yes, yes good music here) they said as if my remark was a profound insight into the nature of Cuban life. "Good", I thought as I turned the corner and went uphill away from them. However, I had watched Olympic Games and I had seen Cuban athletes like Alberto Juantoreno or Figuerola who would have had no trouble catching me if they had decided to sprint after me. With each step I felt safer and then began to feel guilty for assuming that life in Santiago was like the part of Glasgow where I grew up. The music was getting louder and I could see street lighting ahead. Finally, I reached the top of the hill that led down to the Casa Grande. With great relief I strolled down. There was a little crowd on the pavement outside the club. I decided to stop, listen to the music and gather myself. In my relieved state I was only dimly aware of a figure beside me. When I turned I saw a pair of glistening eyes in a very black face. She was a little smaller than I am, aged in her late teens, wearing the kind of bright orange and red dress black women can wear to such effect. "Do you like the music sir?" Her accent was delicate and beguiling. She smiled a little, showing wonderfully white teeth. You really don`t need fluoride in the water, I thought. "Yes, I do. Very much," I replied. "Would you like to make music with me, sir?" she continued quietly. I reflected on what I would have given as a young man to have attracted any attention at all from such a beauty. What made me now so appealing? Personality, charisma, nonchalance, sheer masculine magnetism? No, none of them. "I`m sorry, there is a lady waiting for me back

46

at my hotel and I am late," She smiled a little. "I'll be here tomorrow evening," she said. I walked away, assuming I would remember her longer than she remembered me. I realised I was quite tired when I got into the hotel, crossed the marble floor and took the lift. Mary smiled when I got to the room, a little relieved to see me, I think. "Well, how was it?" "Dreadful." She laughed. She was feeling much better. I suggested a daiquiri and we were happy to relax in the bar.

We flew back to Havana in time to pick up another car, this time a little more aware of the challenges. We were heading for our last destination on the island. This was Pinar del Rio in the north where much of the tobacco is grown for the famous cigars. This time I asked for travel directions from the car hire representative who was sympathetic with our previous difficulties. Again, we received detailed instructions. Again we followed them. This time, they were accurate. We were soon on a wide highway out of Havana. We were not very far along the road when we began to notice little groups of people walking beside the road. Many were trying to hitch a lift from the passing traffic. We saw some cars and vans stop in response. We had read this was common in Cuba but because of the corkscrew path we had followed on our previous trip we had not seen much of it. We saw a young woman with a much older man who looked quite tired. We decided to stop. They were father and daughter and they were very grateful for the lift. It turned out we had saved them from a hike of several miles in hot sun. Again, they were friendly and the girl particularly was keen to know about Britain, David Beckham, what we thought of Cuba and the Beatles. Their village was about a mile off the main highway. They thanked us and offered us coffee. We decided we would rather continue our journey. We felt that if we had challenges ahead we would rather face them in daylight. Their parting shot was that if we returned to Cuba we could stay with them for a dollar a night.

We continued and were much relieved to find the turnoff to Pinar del Rio. Then we were at the mercy of the travel agent`s brochure which gave us directions from the town. Our hotel was a couple of miles outside at Vinales. It was called Horizontes Los Jazmines and the sight of it took our breath away. It is a modern hotel with an outdoor pool. It sits on a wooded hillside overlooking the magnificent valley which stretches all the way to the high mountains of the coast. Our room had a balcony that overlooked the valley where `mogotes`, limestone hills like giant molehills, were scattered across the very green countryside with palm trees in clusters and occasional little cottages. It was the perfect place to end our visit. We spent most of the last couple of days strolling around and I was so inspired by the marvellous panorama of the valley that I attempted one of my amateurish sketches which turned out to be colourful if not accurate.

So, Cuba was magnificent. Given time there was so much more we could have done and happily would have. Our last aim before leaving was to see Hemingway`s house at San Francisco da Paula, just outside Havana. We found San Francisco da Paula and we ate in his favourite local restaurant where, surprisingly, we were regaled with "Dos gardenias, Guantanamera and Chissa, chissa, chissa ", but we never found the house. Locals and policemen sent us one way and another but we failed to find it.It would be so nice to believe that geopolitics would favour the wonderful Cuban people and allow them some of the prosperity and freedom they richly deserve without their losing their unique qualities.

Rhodes

Rhodes was the first of the Greek islands I visited. Quite late in life I formed the notion that I should like to see all of them before I die. It was only later I decided it might be wise to find out how many there were to see what size of task I had set myself. Books vary in their assessment between 1,400 and 3,000. This seemed like a lot and I decided I had to trim my ambitions. It was obviously sensible to ignore all the uninhabited ones, many of which are not much more than rocks in the sea. Then I decided to forget those only inhabited by goats and monks. That was a surprising number. When I then excluded ones inhabited by goats or monks that reduced it still further.

I began with Rhodes for a number of reasons. The primary one was that I could fly there direct from Glasgow at a time that suited me. I had decided to use a tour company called Solo`s which organises holidays for people without partners or whose partners do not want to holiday with them. I had done various trips entirely on my own since the end of my marriage and I didn`t mind doing it. The freedom appealed to me, but I had to admit that the evenings would have been improved by some company to discuss the day`s events. Solo`s offered a viable alternative: company if you wanted it, solitude if you preferred. They also had some attractive excursions on offer. I worried a little that I would be spending a week with some sad people, but that turned out not to be the case.

Our hotel was in Ialysos, a small town just a couple of miles south of the capital city, Rhodes Town, famous as the chosen location for the Knights Templar after the Muslims threw them out of Jerusalem. The Knights Templar have, of course, become the stuff of much fact and fancy down the years and no wonder. Almost everything about them is entirely bizarre. They are thought to have formed in order to protect the Temple of Solomon (hence the name Templar) in Jerusalem. This was located on Temple Mount where Muslims erected the Al-Aqsa mosque. It was also allegedly the site of other events such as Abraham`s encounter with the angel and the ascent of Mahomet into Heaven. The pseudo or real sacred associations pile up as you investigate and it has been described as the holiest place on earth. Considering the fighting and bloodshed that has surrounded that small piece of land it could just as convincingly be considered the unholiest. In any event, once the Muslims retook Jerusalem the Knights had to base themselves elsewhere and Rhodes was the chosen location.

After settling into a bright, comfortable modern hotel overlooking the sea (Aegean I think but one sea seamlessly merges into another in this part of the globe and they`re all part of the Mediterranean) at Ialysos we were invited to a reception where we met our rep and Jimmy the Greek. Our rep was an amazing fellow called Andrew. At first sight the only striking thing about him was his suntan. He looked as if he`d been fired in an oven. As the week wore on we discovered he was a man of unusual stamina, who could drink with the boys in town until 3 in the morning and still turn up for a hearty breakfast before most of us had stirred. Andrew gave us a brief rundown of the attractions of the island: the Venetian Harbour and Templar city in Rhodes town, the Butterfly Farm at Tholos, the citadel at Lindos, and the romantic ruined city of Kamiros. He innocently devastated one of our party who asked if there would be an excursion to see the Colossus, since she had been saving for years to come and photograph the great wonder, having consistently failed to find pictures of it. Andrew gently explained that she was 2,296 years too late, since the amazing 30 metre statue had only stood for 56 years before being destroyed by an earthquake. We have a high regard for the ancient Greeks and their intelligence but the thinking behind erecting a giant statue in iron and bronze in one of the world`s most active earthquake zones is not immediately clear. Her reaction suggested she suspected Andrew of malicious time travel to dismantle the Colossus as an act of spite against her, although he had never previously heard of her.

Then it was the turn of Jimmy the Greek. His name puzzled us a little. How many Greeks are called Jimmy, and why did they need to tell us he was Greek since everyone else in the hotel also was? We were, after all, in Greece. He limped onto the stage on a pair of crutches, result evidently of taking a walk to buy a paper. He didn`t explain any further but perhaps a quick earthquake had got him. He was a stout fellow with amazingly heavy eyelids and a fleshy mouth. His job was to sell the excursions. He described the outings to Lindos and Kamiros in extravagant terms, but saved his Homeric gifts for the voyage to the little island of Symi. At this his eyes became misty and his voice seemed to break a little. He told us that the front at Symi was wonderfully beautiful but the real jewel of the island was the monastery of St. Michael on the other side from the capital. With pauses to deal with the emotional waves he told us that St. Michael's spirit still presided over the lovely monastery, and many well attested miracles had taken place there. "St. Michael will never let you down," he intoned. "When you are there ask him anything, anything and then be prepared to be astonished." Nobody had the nerve to ask him "So, why are you still limping, Jimmy" but we did all wonder how many fridges he had sold to Lappland.

This visit was not long after I had begun to learn modern Greek. I really had no idea when I began what a difficult language it is. This fact draws a mixture of amusement, admiration and pity from Greeks. Since many of them speak acceptable English it's not obvious to them why anyone would bother to learn their language which even exasperates them with its oddities and complications. However, my small and really rather unimpressive achievements in this regard entertained them greatly. Its benefits became quickly clear.

There was no excursion available on our first day so I walked the two miles into Rhodes Town. The road skirted the sea and I walked beneath a bright blue sky with the sun not quite at its hottest. That eventually led me onto a beach which was at the southern end of the modern town. On sighting shops and restaurants I recognised that my caffeine levels were getting dangerously low. There were several cafés along the front. Greek cafés in my experience vary between the traditional ones, often referred to as kafeneios, where old men sit for most of the day smoking, and impressively modern ones with colourful, well upholstered sofas or minimalist high stools. I was very warm from my walk and the temptation to find the coolest shady corner was strong. However, I love looking out to blue skies and sea. I chose a café with small, neat leather chairs and little tables. I settled at one in the shade, still in sight of the beach. The café was quiet but soon a young woman with shoulder length blond hair curling round her ears and neck came over. She was a little fleshy but shapely. Her smile was natural and welcoming. I managed to greet her in her own language which drew a little smile. As I then proceeded to order my coffee in Greek her smile widened. "Bravo," she said in English, suggesting she was not overly impressed. "You are learning Greek. Why are you doing that?" I told her that languages interest me and Greek seemed like a challenge. She nodded as if she didn`t quite believe me, served me coffee and then refused payment for it.

I went on to find the historic town. I approached the impressive entrance gate with interest and anticipation. Most of the building dates from the 14th century when the knights moved in. They remained for two hundred years before the Turks drove them out. The Avenue of the Knights which consists of `inns` devoted to each of the seven countries that offered manpower remains a very impressive street, now largely occupied by offices. I went on from there to see the rest of the old town which was in excellent condition and suggested a group of men with with taste in architecture and a fair grasp of how to live well. The weather in Rhodes is beautiful. There would have been ample wine, fruit, fish and olives. Perhaps not difficult to see why young men might have abandoned some of the pestilential slums of mediaeval Europe on a wet November afternoon for this. I left with the firm intention of discovering more about these enigmatic knights.

However, the abundance of sheer nonsense written about them has so far deterred me from carrying that out.

We then had our first excursion, a coach trip to some of the main sights of the island. Our guide was to be a very lovely young Athenian named Anne Marie whose mastery of English impressed me all the more when I learned she had never visited an English speaking country. We went first of all to Kamiros which was once the principal town of the island. It was largely destroyed by earthquakes in the third and second centuries B.C but the ruins still give a clear idea of the layout. It sits on the western coast on a gentle slope running down to the sea. As always in old Greek towns the highest point is occupied by the temple or Acropolis, which means `the top of the town`. From there it runs down almost to the coast, a neatly laid out town where shops, markets and fine houses all once existed. Anne Marie gave us a lucid account of its construction and what life must have been like. This was not altogether easy since one of our party was a round Glaswegian (I am also Glaswegian) with a voice several octaves below basso profundo and a tendency to relate the world to parts of Glasgow. He interrupted our guide with a question: "That street looks like one in Maryhill that goes down to the railway. Would they have had a railway?" Anne Marie hesitated for a moment, almost imperceptibly, as she wondered whether this might be some form of alien humour. One look at the furrowed brow and the blank eyes confirmed that he wasn`t joking. Gently, she pointed out that this had been built almost three thousand years before the first steam engine and even today there were no railways on Rhodes. He seemed to have a follow-up question but mercifully one of the women inquired about the Greek language and whether it had three genders. Anne-Marie confirmed it had but explained they were not always logical since the normal word for a dog was usually neuter. Our Glaswegian saw his chance and rumbled "Why did they neuter their dogs then?"We travelled from there through very green countryside to Petaloudes or Butterfly Valley, This is a delightfully shaded, wooded area by a stream. In fact it has no butterflies at all but is a major breeding site for the Panaxaria moth. It was simply decided that `butterfly` sounds more endearing and less spooky than `moth` and anyway, even the one biologist in our group was not at all sure what the difference is. Sadly the moths are in steep decline for a strange reason. The adult moth has no stomach. It only survives by the energy it built up as a caterpillar. The large number of visitors disturbs them and makes them fly around more than they should, using up their scarce reserves. The valley was cool and still. Even without stomachs the moths, I felt, had taste.

From there we went up Mount Attavyros which, at 1215 metres is the island`s highest peak. We didn`t go to the summit but stopped at the town of Embonas, the hub of Rhodes` wine-growing area. Anne- Marie, like guides I had come across throughout southern Europe, was adept at reciting the advantages of the local produce. I don`t have a very discriminating palate for wine and I certainly never feel like drinking it in the late morning so I can`t really say how good it was. As always on these occasions, the bus emptied as if snakes had appeared on it and infirm ladies who had climbed aboard with difficulty showed impressive speed to join the queue. Busy as Anne-Marie appeared to be, our Glaswegian felt she would benefit from the knowledge that: "we make whisky in Scotland and you get different whisky in Islay from what you get on the Spey...." Martin, a quiet but pleasant London truck driver advised me that the red Cava Emery was a good choice. Evidently wine was a hobby of his. He and his mates often went to wine tastings so he apparently knew a bit about it. "Ye see, the difference is the water..." I heard my fellow Glaswegian intone with, as far as I could tell, no one listening.

Jimmy the Greek returned to our hotel that evening, still, by all appearances, being ignored by St. Michael. One of the other subjects about which he became emotional was "the completely unfair reputation given to Faliraki". It was true that most of us had heard it was the one place on the island that should be avoided unless you are an alcoholic teenager who doesn`t mind being assaulted, or waking up with one or more people you can`t name and may not even like. Jimmy alleged that this reputation had come from one misinformed TV programme. We doubted that. However, he prevailed upon the more credulous of us to go along to "a wonderful restaurant" in the town so we could appreciate how beautiful and friendly it is. In fact the restaurant was good and friendly, but on the way back one of the ladies had her handbag stolen and another was narrowly missed by a flying bottle. The lady got her handbag back when we all set off in pursuit of the culprit who, I feel, overrated the sprinting power of our party and abandoned the goods. Sadly, as with everything else we`d heard about the town`s shortcomings, the fellow was British.

The last excursion was to the delightful, tiny island of Symi. Symi is far nearer the Turkish coast than anything Greek and it is one of these anomalies of political history that Greece owns it. Most of us took this trip, several hoping St. Michael was good with hangovers. In fact the monastery was beautiful and impressive. Some people lingered, possibly with a long list for the saint. I noticed there was a tiny café attached, overlooking the sea. After appreciating the fine building and its atmosphere I decided to enjoy the sunshine. Two ladies served. One was a quiet but smiling dark-haired woman. The other was a severe looking older one. I thought I`d make her day by ordering in Greek. She glared at me silently for a moment and then said "What are you wanting?" in a tone that suggested working so close to a holy place was a strain on the nerves. I said "coffee" but before I managed to define whether I wanted espresso, Americano, latte, skinny latte, mocha or any other variation she splashed boiling water into a mug with a sprinkling of Nescafé at the bottom. She then squirted some evaporated milk into it and glared at me again in a "well are you going to pay me or do I have to take hostile action?" type of manner. I handed over a euro and retreated to the sunshine, wondering if Michael could manage a quick thunderbolt.

After an hour at the monastery the boat took us round to the town for lunch. The bay was as picturesque as in most of these Greek islands and mainland harbours. Houses in orange, pink, blue and white all clustered merrily at the front and open air restaurants bustled with trade. Andrew led us to one where we sat at two long tables. The waiter, whom I took also to be the owner, chatted smilingly to us, glad to explain the menu in very acceptable English. He was around forty, I guessed, a little overweight but with the right kind of easy but efficient manner. I always like to try menu items which I have never tasted before so when I saw `sea snails` as an option I thought that would be interesting. "No, don`t take them," instructed the waiter. I was surprised. "Why not?"

 "Because you won`t like them". "How do you know?" I questioned. "Nobody does," he replied. It occurred to me to ask why they were on offer at all, but decided not to pursue it. Maybe he served them as a treat to customers he didn`t want to see again.

My week on Rhodes was excellent. I liked the island very much and could happily return. Once I`ve done the other 1399 islands perhaps I shall.

North West Greece

My latest Solo`s trip was to Parga on the north west coast of
Greece. It is a short boat trip from the islands of Corfu, Paxos
and Antipaxos. I had never heard of Parga until a few weeks
earlier but it is unquestionably one of the most beautiful places I
have ever seen. Our hotel was on the beach which curved round
to be flanked on the hills on either side by a castle, one Turkish
and one Venetian. Each was beautifully illuminated at night,
making a spectacular setting with the lights reflected in the
indigo water in the bay. A short walk which included a
breathtaking(in both senses) steep climb past the Venetian castle
led to the little town. In typical Greek style it consisted of
attractive buildings which looked like an advert for a paint box.
The colours were bold, vivid and gave the scene a delightful,
toytown effect as if we had wandered into the ideal world of a
child`s imagination. Along the front were traditional tavernas and
more modern cafés and bars. They looked out on the deep blue
bay which usually had little white boats in it along with the
occasional vessel straight from Pirates of the Caribbean. Some of
the characters who strode along the pier were not that far from
Captain Sparrow. In the distance we could see the dim shapes of
Corfu and Paxos.

I decided to take all the excursions I could. The first was to
`Greek Ruins`. This was not in fact about the modern economy
but began with a trip to the wonderfully named Necromanteio,
evocative of the `necromancy` of modern English which we use

to mean witchcraft. The name is a combination of `necro` (dead) and `mantevo` (to guess or divine). The bus parked in the town and we walked up another steep hill to an ancient temple, allegedly 4,000 years old, now a ruin, but still impressive with huge polygonal stones and no mortar or cement. Green landscape stretched to nearby mountains on one side and the sea on the other. The learned guide explained to us that to the west we were looking at the delta of the river Acheron (or Styx) which the ancient Greeks believed came from the Underworld, Hades. On the other side, only a few hundred metres away were the ancient Elysian Fields or Paradise. That pleasant but unremarkable area had given rise to so many poetic musings in so many languages down the centuries as well as the ultra sophisticated Champs Elysees of modern Paris. We entered the temple. In ancient times people would come there from far and wide to speak to the dead. Even then they had the strange view, still prevalent, that their late auntie whose advice they regularly ignored in life was suddenly worth listening to just because she`s dead. When they arrived they had to answer a questionnaire offered by an Iron Age receptionist. This supplied extensive information about their lives, dead relatives, health etc. This was passed to the priests. Visitors were then given a meal of some kind of meat with vinegar and broad beans. This made them feel rather ill. That was followed by extract of magic mushroom. Sick and hallucinating they were then led down to `the Underworld`, a stone chamber which would have been filled with smoke. Amid the smoke they would have seen the dark faces of the dead which were actually masks held by the priests. Visitors were then invited to ask questions of their dead relatives. Since, from the questionnaire, the priests knew all about them, the answers astonished the deluded visitors with the detail about their lives. Any prophecy would have been sufficiently ambiguous to have meant anything. This is presumably one of the earliest recorded scams, though

61

possibly some of the Bible ones are older. Human nature doesn`t change very much.

We then went through very attractive green and mountainous scenery to a kafeneio, a café in a little mountain village where you could get coffee of indifferent quality along with rather a good spinach pie. This was spacious and pleasant where you could sit in the shade of trees and watch the old men you find in every Greek café with apparently nothing else to do.

After that we went to the sad but impressive site of Salongo, famous to every modern Greek. It was the site of a mass suicide of women and children pursued up a steep hillside by Turkish soldiers whose grasp of courtesy and chivalry was imperfect. The huge white monument was visible from afar. Greece, like other east European countries, has not been lucky in its choice of neighbours.

The day ended with a trip to the source of the River Styx at Gliki (which is Greek for sweet or sweets since it is plural). It is the term for fresh water which bubbles up in a multitude of tiny springs in the impressive gorge which is the riverbed. This is, allegedly, where Achilles` mother, Thetis, dangled her young son to make him immortal and invincible. Famously, she held him by the heel thus leading to his death from the arrow fired by Paris, possibly guided by Apollo. I paddled in the river which is not very deep. It only came up to my knees. I am therefore now immortal from the knees down. Not quite sure how that works when my number`s up but if you ever see a pair of shins with feet wandering around you will know the answer. I have known people dead from the neck up but not from the knees.

This trip had involved getting up at 6 in the morning. The following morning I got up at 5 and sacrificed breakfast to get on the bus for Meteora which I have always wanted to see. This amazing site on the edge of the plane of Thessaly beside the little town of Kalabaka in central Greece consists of six monasteries built on rock towers which shoot out of the landscape to a height of 700 metres at the highest. The first of these astonishing buildings was constructed by the monk Athanasios in the fourteenth century. How he got up the sheer cliff face is a mystery (repeated with more help and technology by Roger Moore as James Bond in `For your Eyes Only`). I had seen photographs of this site but could never quite believe it. In reality it was no less impressive. We were allowed inside the oldest and largest of the monasteries .It was very beautiful with structure which both from the point of view of aesthetics and durability could well have taught lessons to those who put up the new Standard Life headquarters in Edinburgh. Those who think that money talks should give thought to what people will do when inspired by thoughts of eternal life (not just from the knees down).

The cliffs of Meteora are all the more impressive since they are set against the wide plane of Thessaly, home of the aforesaid Achilles and his shameful Myrmidons who dragged Hector `s corpse around the walls of Troy.

The following day I had a more restful time. I rose at eight and had a good breakfast before joining the others (the only trip any of the others took) on the boat to the nearby islands of Paxos and Antipaxos. This involved a voyage of about one hour across the Ionian Sea. We only had time to visit the main town of each . Lunch in a pretty seaside restaurant in Antipaxos produced one of the worst omelettes I have ever come across. Later in Paxos we settled in one of the many modern, appealing cafés and enjoyed a small beer in the 30 degree afternoon sun.

Not yet ready to idle on the beach, the following day I took the service bus down to Preveza from which I took another bus to Levkas (an island joined by a short causeway to the mainland) to meet my friend and Greek teacher, Nikos, who normally lives in Edinburgh but was holidaying in his homeland. I had estimated the bus should take about an hour and a quarter to get to Preveza. However, I thought it might detour to some of the villages so I left more than two and a half hours to be sure of catching my connection in Preveza. The bus trip was like a caricature of Greek life. The large, bearlike driver with a head of very Greek-hero looking dark curls but a body which was no stranger to chips and beer stopped at every village, had a coffee and a cigarette with his pals, yawned, stretched then ,when stuck for further entertainment, climbed in, drove off to do the same at the next settlement. Mercifully, I got my connection with seven minutes to spare. Nikos and I had a good lunch and were then joined by two young Greek women, Thora and Thespina, who were friends of his. We had a walk by the sea and then Thora drove us back to my bus, a trip that let me understand Nikos` view that the absolute proof that there is a God is that Thora is still alive and not long since wiped out in a traffic accident.

I felt I had now earned a little idleness. In the last two days I strolled into town, had very good coffee in the café of the Venetian castle and interrogated a number of tavern owners which resulted in two supremely good lunches on sea bream and sea bass with fresh vegetables and aubergine salad. Altogether a great experience. I like Greece. The food and the coffee can vary but with a little effort and discrimination you can find good examples of both.

Greece is a troubled country. There have not been many phases of its history when this has not been the case. However, I have found it a delightful one. It is an irony often quoted that the

64

country that gave us democracy is not a great example of it. Its politicians have not served it well. The immense borrowing which has crippled the economy has given rise to a number of important questions. Where has all the money gone? How culpable have some of its elected politicians been? How did the country move from no significant debt when democracy returned in 1974 after the colonels` junta to one with debts of 180% of GDP. Equally, why did foreign banks and governments lend to it so imprudently? However, it is a very beautiful country with great variety in a very small area. Its many islands add to this great variety and its people, in my experience, are friendly and humorous although they do like an argument. Its crime rate is very low with perhaps the lowest murder rate in Europe. There is no doubt it has a rich class which can be very autocratic and selfish and that poses problems, but they are not alone in that. I would urge anyone having to visit it and enjoy its many attractions.

About the Author

Robert Noble Graham had a career in the oil, publishing and finance industries. He is a graduate in French and German and in English. He is divorced with two adult children, both scientists. He has written drama that has been produced on BBC Radio 4 and in Scottish theatres. He has contributed specialist financial articles to various journals and is a regular contributor to Mensa magazine. He lives in Scotland and is the author of three published novels:

The Celebrity of Anders Hecht, Masks of Venice,

The Women from Crete

Made in the USA
Middletown, DE
21 October 2020